MASTERING VIDEO PRODUCTION:

Techniques and Tips for Creating
Professional-Quality Content

JUNAID AHMED

ISBN-13: 9798374541915

Publishing Support by Amazel Enterprise
Cover and Interior Design by: Arbëresh Dalipi
www.amazelenterprise.com
publishingsupport@amazelenterprise.com

+1868 346 8616

Dedication

"This book is dedicated to my family, who have been my greatest supporters and inspirations throughout my journey as a videographer and photographer. To my uncle, who introduced me to the world of film cameras and sparked my love for visual storytelling. To my dad, who introduced me to the camcorder and sparked my passion for capturing life's precious moments. And to my wife, who gave me my first iPhone and my first DSLR camera, and has been by my side every step of the way. Thank you for your unwavering support and encouragement, this book is for you."

My Introduction to Video Production

I am excited to get into strategies for success with mobile video production for the iPhone. All my life I've been passionate about mobile video production.
First, let's take a walk down memory lane as I share with you where it all began.

Family TV Time

Growing up, watching TV was a treat. We had many responsibilities that took priority over watching TV, so we had a strict schedule of just 30 minutes, Monday through Friday, at 5pm. This was the most exciting time of the day for us. We mostly watched cartoons at first, but as we got older, we were introduced to American TV shows like Full House and Knight Rider. Even today, these shows hold a special place in my memory.

Curious Junaid

How did I get into video creation? What inspired me?

Watching these TV shows sparked a passion in me for the entertainment industry.
I became fascinated with the process of creating a film or TV show and dove
deeper into researching the different steps involved. I was particularly drawn to
the stories and the technology used to bring them to life.
I had so many questions, like how did they create the special effects?
How did they make everything look so realistic?

Coming to America

I first visited the United States when I was 9 years old, and then again when I was 13. Both trips were during summer break from Saudi Arabia and they were truly epic experiences. Most of my family lived in the US, so I was able to spend time with them and explore the country. Each time we had to leave, I cried. I missed my cousins, aunts and uncles tremendously. During my visits, I was exposed to a wide variety of movies and I loved it. I watched so many films and added a few of them to my all-time favorite list, such as "Back to the Future," "Ghostbusters," "E.T," and "The Never-Ending Story." These movies left a lasting impression on me and solidified my interest in technology.

Father Sharing The Gift

When I was 19 years old, my father received a video camera as a recognition award for being with the company for 15 years. He was a Systems Analyst. It was a Canon camcorder that used a Hi8 8mm videotape. At first, the camera was not allowed to be used by anyone because it was considered a novelty item. I didn't give it much thought at the time because I was preoccupied with a camera an uncle had given me. Interestingly, this uncle would soon become my mentor. I also had goals to accomplish, as my father would only allow me to go to America if I met them, otherwise, I would be sent to Pakistan. I kept focused and was able to move to the US shortly after. It wasn't until a couple of years later when my siblings came to America that I saw the full recording capabilities of that camcorder. They brought footage they had captured with them. It consisted of scenes they created which were really quite entertaining to watch. It was then that I realized the potential of that camera and how it could be used for storytelling and filmmaking.

Junaid The Little Technician

At the age of 25 my mother brought my father's camcorder to the United States when she migrated. I finally had the opportunity to use it and I spent a lot of time trying to understand how it worked and how to create good videos. I never took any classes on videography, I just experimented and had fun with it. I remember one time when my siblings and I shot scenes in a similar style to the movie "The Blair Witch Project". You should have seen us running around the park. It was sensational!

The Tech Junkie

That year when I got a job as a web and UI designer and developer, I had the chance to use a Sony Cybershot DSC-F717 camera with a 5x optical zoom lens. My boss said I could use it since he didn't use it very often. The camera could take 5-megapixel photos. Believe it or not, I still have some of those pictures. I was happy to be able to combine my interests in computers and photography. Additionally, in hindsight the influence of seeing an entrepreneur run his business did have an impact on my life.

The Mentor - Respect

I distinctly remember taking apart two computers and putting them back together. Learning how to connect things positioned me for growth in this field. The videographer with whom I began working with years after was the same person who I would build computers for at another job. He then had a wedding photography and videography business. I asked if I could help and he said yes. This enabled me to see the process and behind-the-scenes of what he was doing and the quality of the footage that was created. This is how I got introduced to video editing using software applications such as Adobe Premiere, Sony Vegas, and others. He used Adobe Premiere along with some specific transitions.

Junaid The Problem Solver

As I got more involved in helping with the video shoots and editing, I became increasingly interested in the process. I noticed that a lot of the rendering of the edited videos (compilations) required a lot of CPU processing and it would take a lot of time to render. We often had to wait for hours to make sure the final product was what we intended. This presented a problem, and I believed I could fix it by building faster computers. I did so and soon we were able to render videos in half the time.

Junaid The Family Videographer

The camera, which my father received as a gift from his employer, was more than just a device for recording; it was a tool for creating lasting memories and connecting with the people I love. Its flip-out screen allowed me to compose shots with intention, while its viewfinder helped me fine-tune each moment. The camcorder used Hi8 8mm video tapes, and it had optical zoom and auto-focus to keep the subjects sharp, which were standard features in most camcorders at the time. This camera, like my father, was a gift that kept on giving, and it continued to inspire me to pursue my passion for videography.

The Budget Challenges

As my career as a web designer and user experience/user interface designer progressed, I also got married. However, keeping up with the latest technology in videography was difficult due to the cost of equipment. But then, the introduction of the iPhone revolutionized the field, opening up endless possibilities and making it more accessible to people, forever changing the way we approached videography.

My First iPhone with Video

The first iPhone was released in the United States in June 2007. My wife gifted me with my first iPhone, the 8GB version, for my birthday present at the launch date. I was blown away by this thoughtful gesture, as there is always something extra special about the first of anything. This was a dream come true.

Each iPhone upgrade brought new and exciting features.

In the fall of 2013, Apple introduced the iPhone 5S, which allowed for 1080p video recording. This was a game changer, as I could not only shoot video on the iPhone, but also edit, add titles, and publish to popular video sites with ease. I had been a big supporter of Kickstarter campaigns, and had backed a wide-angle lens that, when combined with the iPhone 5S, allowed me to shoot extensive videos. In 2015, I captured an off-roading trip in the hills of Utah and edited and published it on my YouTube channel, where it gained 34K views. The video was named "Fins and Things." With the iPhone, the possibilities are endless, we are no longer bound to the desktop or laptop.

Creating Video that Resonates

Creating a video that effectively communicates your message and resonates with your audience can seem like a daunting task, but with the right approach, it can be done with ease. In this guide, we will be discussing the various steps involved in mobile video production using an iPhone. The iPhone is the perfect device for mobile video production as it is equipped with advanced technology and offers a wide range of apps to help you create professional-grade videos.

We will be going over the technical aspects of mobile video production, including the tools and equipment needed, as well as best practices for filming, editing and publishing your video. So, whether you're a beginner or an experienced video creator, this guide will provide you with the knowledge and resources you need to take your mobile video production to the next level.

Basic Fundamentals

Before we begin delving into the technical aspects of mobile video production, it's important to make sure you have the necessary tools and equipment ready. Here are some essential items to have on hand to ensure your shoot goes smoothly.

1. Storage

This first tip is very important. We're constantly taking pictures and videos on our iPhones. Sometimes we tend to forget about this. It is why professional photographers carry a bag full of it. STORAGE!!! The storage on your device is very important. Make sure you have at least 10 to 16 GB free on your device. Having less space affects the ability of the operating system to process efficiently.

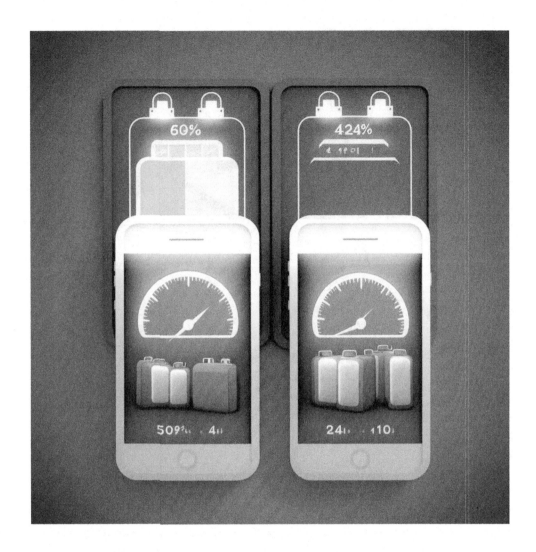

11. Battery

You want to make sure there is enough battery power on your device. A full battery is a lifesaver. Especially when you see the clouds moving and you want to capture the movement of the clouds by doing the time-lapse. Every time you travel, make sure that your battery is fully charged for use.

III. Video Compression

Based on storage, let's say you have 30-45 free minutes and you want to capture those amazing clouds rolling by, but you only have 5 gigs of storage space available and your battery life is at 40%. Video compression settings can help you in this situation by using less storage space and less battery life, so you may be able to get that footage. Compression helps in these tight spots and since most shots are around 5-10 seconds, your clean shots will blend seamlessly with other footage in the final composition. For more information on compression, check out the video resolution section in the Essential Unit.

IV. Preparation

One of the key points that we often overlook is preparation. It may take just a few minutes for us to prepare for our daily routine, but when creating a brand new video, we have to think, contemplate and devise the best way to deliver the message to our audience. With a limited time frame to convey the message, preparation is even more crucial.

V. Airplane Mode

Have you ever started recording a video only to be interrupted by a phone call or text message? I'm sure you have. The simplest solution to this problem is to use Airplane Mode. This will send all of your calls temporarily to voicemail, allowing you to capture your thoughts in peace. Airplane mode is also recommended when capturing a time-lapse. Now that we have taken care of these basics, let's dive in and take a look at the first step in creating a successful mobile video.

Video Production Essentials

The following provides an overview of the basics of how a camera functions and what to consider when shooting video. It covers the importance of lighting and adjusting the aperture, shutter speed and ISO to achieve the desired result. It also touches on the concepts of manual mode, aperture and iris, and the importance of understanding the camera settings to capture good footage.

1. Illuminate with Lighting

Let's consider some of the basics of how a camera functions and what you can expect. The camera in your hand has a lot of power, but it also has some drawbacks, particularly with the size of the sensor. If you look at the camera module, it is smaller than your fingertip, and the sensor is even smaller. When shooting video, it is important to ensure there is ample light and not to overpower the sensor. If the images appear washed out, it is a sign that there is too much light and the aperture on the lens should be adjusted to allow less light in.

The aperture on the lens of a camera functions similarly to the iris of our eyes. Our eyes have pupils that dilate and shrink, which determines how much light enters our eyes. At night, the pupils dilate to allow more light to enter, but during the day, the pupils shrink to let in less light. A camera lens operates in the same way, with the aperture being the opening and the aperture number corresponding to the iris, which is the sensor.

When the aperture is opened fully, a lot of light enters. To compensate for this, the camera increases the shutter speed. Most of the time, the camera is set to manual mode, allowing for greater control of the settings. In this mode, you can observe the numbers and adjust the shutter speed, ISO and other settings to achieve the desired results.

When filming, consider the available light, the time of day, and whether additional lighting is needed. Also, be sure to use your device correctly and learn the basics, this will take you a long way in capturing good footage.

11. Focus on Sound

The second most important thing in video production is sound. It is essential to ensure that the audio in your video is clear and easily heard. There are several ways to achieve this, such as using a dedicated microphone, a lavalier microphone, or an external audio device. Additionally, many smartphones, such as the iPhone, have built-in features that make capturing sound easy and accurate. The iPhone, for example, has three microphones: one by the mouthpiece, one by the ear, and one next to the rear-facing camera. These microphones work together to cancel out ambient noise and enhance the audio signals in the video.

However, in some cases, such as when recording an interview in a crowded place, it may be necessary to use external audio recorders or a long cable to directly connect the audio source to your device.

III. Optimal Orientation

The third item you should consider is the orientation of your device. There has been a debate for the past decade about which orientation is best for video recording; it wasn't debated before because the general public could only record video horizontally. Initially, it was more like a square, but as technology evolved, the video aspect ratio became broader, more extensive, and more horizontal, capturing landscape views.

Orientation is fundamental, but modern technology and the ability to record video on smartphones have expanded so that you can now record video in portrait mode, vertical, or horizontal, or landscape orientation. Additionally, an accessible format introduced by Instagram, the square video, works on every platform and in many applications. While landscape orientation is the default and the industry standard used by all movie and TV production filmmakers, it's important to consider where your audience will be watching the video and choose the appropriate orientation for them.

Vertical orientation was not widely accepted in the beginning, but then smartphones were able to record video. We even had vertical video PSA's - Public Service Announcements, about why you should not shoot vertical video. Long story short (pun!), vertical orientation is now legit, and it can be used to shoot videos specifically for creating Instagram or Facebook stories. It gets your message across the board, where it can be viewed by people consuming on these vast, prevalent social networks.

Which format do you use? Which orientation do you shoot your video in? Where are they going to be watching this video? It all comes down to the location of your targeted audience. The answer determines how you would create the video and the appropriate orientation.

IV. Stabilization Methods

Anytime you're shooting video in either orientation, you want to make sure that you're using a proper stabilization method. You can either set your phone down on the counter, mount it on a tripod, or attach it to a device that will keep it leveled. There are several ways that you can go about stabilizing your iPhone. The number one method of stabilizing your iPhone to record video is by using a tripod.

There is a secondary means of stabilizing your footage after you've finished shooting. This involves some software manipulation with software that can stabilize your footage in the application, such as Adobe After Effects. Final Cut Pro and Adobe Premier also offer this capability to stabilize your shot to a certain extent. This means that when using software stabilization methods, the only potential drawback is that some of the footage might be cropped or zoomed in on the subject, which could result in losing some of the original footage.

V. Video Resolution & Aspect Ratio

There are a few video resolutions that are the industry standards for film and television, but the ones we're going to focus on are enabled by default. On the iPhone Camera app, you have a few options. This falls in line with the compression of the video and how much storage it uses on your device. All of these resolutions are locked in at a 16:9 aspect ratio unless you record a square video then it is 1:1.

Along with the resolution you also want to know how much storage you're using as you record these videos, below you can see how much space a minute of video will use on your device:

- 60 MB with 720p HD at 30 fps "space saver" 1280x720
- 130 MB with 1080p at 30 fps "standard" 1920x1080
- 175 MB with 1080p at 60 fps "smoother video, more on this later"
- 270 MB with 4K at 24 fps "film style" 3840x2160
- 350 MB with 4K at 30 fps "higher resolution"
- 400 MB with 4K at 60 fps "higher resolution and smoother"

What do these numbers and letters all mean? Well, when shooting your video, you want to record at the highest resolution possible, but also know what the standard default is, this will be set to 1080p 30fps as it is the industry standard for video.

The frames per second decide how many frames or snaps or pictures are stored in one second of video captured. A higher frame rate will give you a very smooth video and you can even slow it down a bit for a light "slow-mo" effect.

By understanding the type of storage you are using, you can plan ahead and make sure you have enough space for your videos in the future. The aspect ratio 16:9 (landscape) is the standard used by televisions and most laptop screens, so a full-screen landscape video will fit perfectly on these screens.

The reason to choose the highest resolution possible is to future-proof your content and be able to share it on multiple platforms. Having a higher source video leads to a better export video. Both YouTube and Vimeo support the higher 4K video format, however, social media sites such as Facebook, LinkedIn, and Instagram only support 720p content in either orientation.

VI. Storyboarding

Storyboarding is a crucial step in the video production process, as it allows you to visualize and plan the visual composition of each scene. It is essential for both storytelling videos and talking-head videos as it helps you to organize and illustrate the subject matter you'll be discussing, ensuring that your content is well-structured and on-topic. By creating a storyboard, you can prepare ahead of time and avoid making last-minute changes.

So what's the best way to layout your storyboard? One way to do this is by sketching out your scenes in a notebook and adding details as you develop your content. Additionally, there are various storyboarding software options available that come with pre-made characters, objects, and other features that can be used to enhance your storyboard, but may require additional time to learn how to use them properly. Ultimately, the goal is to create a clear and cohesive visual representation of your story to effectively communicate your message to your audience.

Recommended Apps and Gear

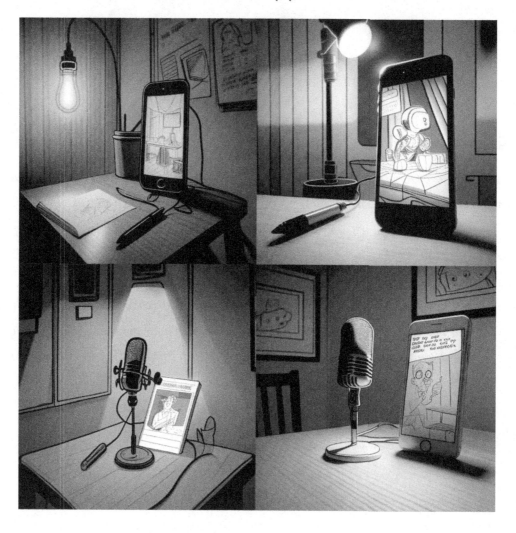

Now that you've learned the fundamentals and essentials of video production, let us look at the application and gear available to you.

Here is a list of applications (apps) and gear that I use and recommend for creating high-quality videos for extended engagement on your social media platforms.

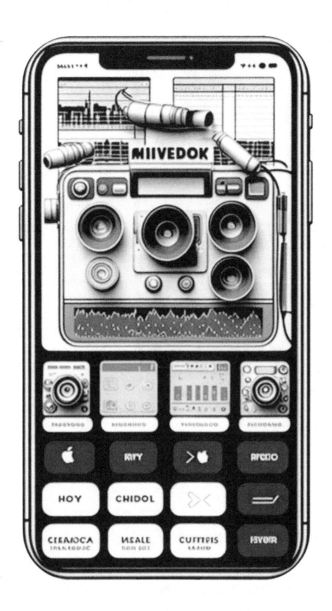

1. Camera Apps

Camera apps enable you to capture video to your device. There are a few options from the level of granularity and clarity you'd like to define.

A. Clips

Clips was introduced by Apple in April 2017 with the release of iOS 10.3 and designed for devices with 64-bit cpus (all iOS devices since 2014 and onwards sport a 64-bit cpu). The Clips app is designed for "making and sharing fun videos with text, effects, graphics, and more," which means it has a lot of features that make it super easy to create videos.

One of the most amazing features built into the Clips app is its ability to convert your voice into text for captions on the fly. As you record your video, SIRI transcribes your audio into text (which is later editable). This is an excellent, awesome feature and creates automatic captioning for you.

Now, most videos are a collection of clips, so this app enables you to create multiple clips as you put them together, edit and trim those bits and come away with a neat-looking video to share with your audience.

Once you've finished recording your video, in the Clips app you can edit your captions. Make sure the spelling of the words that you were saying is correct; 95% of the time the transcription of the text comes out clearly. Other times, you do need to help it a little. It is a fantastic feature built into the Clips app. The app works great on iPhones from 6 to the latest as well on iPad Pro, iPad 9.7 inch, and iPad Mini.

Here is a list of some of the things you can do with this application.

- You can have generated banners added at the beginning, middle, or towards the end of the video.

- You can add photos and rearrange them in the timeline.

- You can insert all the videos that are on your phone.

- It doesn't matter if your video is shot in landscape or portrait; Clips converts all videos into square videos. So, you're either chopping off the left and right of your video or the top and bottom of the video because the meat of the video is usually in the center square.

The best part of Clips is its ability to quickly put "clips". You can then add a soundtrack from a free library to your video, and you're good to go.

There are some hidden features on the Clips app when you're using some of the flagship devices from Apple, such as the iPad Pro with Face ID, the iPhone X, the iPhone XS and XS Max, and the iPhone XR. The FaceID camera enables you to present yourself in a virtual environment.

These "virtual environments" are called Scenes and you'll notice this tab if you're using one of the flagship devices. The scene captures your face from the front-facing camera and replaces the background with one of the sceneries you selected. These scenes include the Millenium Falcon, Nemo, and Dory, the Factory (scare) floor from Monsters, Inc. or you could be a subject drawn in a pencil-drawn sketch world.

There are many more sceneries and new scenes are added every day. The least expensive option for you to consider is the iPhone XR, but the iPad Pro 11-inch is also a great buy because you can do a lot more on the iPad Pro.

B. Camera app

The standard camera app is quick to launch directly from the lock screen and hence it becomes one of the first camera apps that you'll use. Anytime you want to capture photos or videos for later editing, it's an excellent app. Make sure that you have the default settings for your camera app dialed in on the settings section so every time you're shooting video, you're getting consistent results.

C. Filmic Pro (paid) & Filmic Remote

Filmic Pro is one of the most powerful video recording apps you'll encounter; you can change every aspect of the video recording experience. It's one of the apps that have been used by Hollywood-level directors and producers to bring creation to the public. Here is a short list of its functions:

- Manual & Auto zoom & focus
- Quick video format and aspect ratio selection
- Ability to connect with external microphones
- Be controlled remotely from another iOS device
- Zebra lines to help with focus
- Custom LUTs so you can load special color and luma tables to match prior footage or sync up with multiple cameras/iPhones.

11. Video Editing Apps

There are several editing apps available in thapp store. Which one you use entirely depends on you, but I'll list out some of the ones that I've used and recommend.

A. Clips

Clips as mentioned above is an all-encompassing app where it can record & edit video, add layered graphics, as well as banners and titles. To edit in the Clips app, you can bring in the content through 2 sections, the built-in camera (so you're recording video in the app) or bring in clips from videos that are already on your device.

The interesting way this app works to bring content from your camera roll is by enabling you to "record to the timeline" by selecting a video and pressing record (so you can bring in the clip based on the length you're interested in). This is how you set the in and out points from videos on your camera roll.

Once the clip is on the timeline, you can apply further edits but trim the beginning and end of the clip. Also, mute the audio of the clip or keep it, as well as apply effects and stickers to each individual clip.

A. iMovie

iMovie was introduced for iOS alongside the initial release with iPhone 4 in 2010. iPhone 4 was the first iPhone to be able to record 1080p video at 30 fps, so the iMovie paired with it enabled users to edit video on the device. There were a few filmmakers that jumped on and shot some creative short films, including one with the iPhone mounted on a model train chugging along the track. The camera size made it the perfect device to shoot some genius camera angles.

The filmmaker had claimed to have spent 14-24 hours in the iMovie app editing the shots captured on the iPhone. This movie is called "Apple of My Eye" and can be watched on this URL: https://vimeo.com/12819723 with over a million views. The video has been online since 2010.

iMovie app has grown up with the iPhone adding more features, but mainly keeping it super simple to edit your footage and supporting the latest video codecs and formats which the newer and newer iPhones can record in. In 2011, support for iPad 2 was added to iMovie so we could easily edit videos on the bigger screen.

To begin in iMovie, there are two different ways: a Movie or a Trailer. In the movie path, you're open to selecting any number of videos, photos, and music to make your video. This will be the most likely standard way that you might create your videos on this app.The second path is Trailer which gives you 14 templates to choose from and each template tells you the number of cast members that'll be in your trailer. Some trailers have none, and others have 1, 2, or 2-6. The app then walks you through a storyboard and tells you exactly the types of shots you need to make this trailer a reality. All of these trailers are between 59 seconds to 1m 34s. But the end result depends on how many video clips you've added to the trailer.

B. VideoLeap by Enlight

I discovered this app through the app store and through a photo editing app by Enlight called Fotofox. I'm always looking for the best apps out there to make my work easier and more efficient.

With VideoLeap you have a lot more control over how your videos come out. The one item that's a plus over iMovie is the ability to edit and put together portrait-shot videos. If you've ever tried to edit a Vertical video on iMovie, your result will always be a Square video, or with black bars on either side.

With VideoLeap you can start a project by importing videos, choose the format/aspect ratio of your project and get to putting together your masterpiece. This is especially important since many of the social apps such as Instagram, Snapchat, Facebook, TikTok (formerly Musically), and now YouTube will accept vertical videos for visual storytelling. These "stories" are designed to bring your audience a bit closer to you, inviting them to come to check out your profile, website or other call-to-actions.

VideoLeap is a free download with a lot of free features available. They also have a subscription package that'll unlock features like unlimited text layers, effects and new additions that are automatically updated monthly/weekly.

C.   Other Notable Video Editing apps

Here are additional notable video editing apps that are available on the app store:

- Splice and Quik by GoPro
- Adobe Premiere Clip
- Adobe Premiere Rush
- InShot Video Editor
- KineMaster
- Horizon Camera (a genius way to record video, where it eliminates the need to stabilize your camera)
- Magisto – The Smart Video Editor enabling AI to create videos, this editor will upload your videos to its server to create a compelling video.

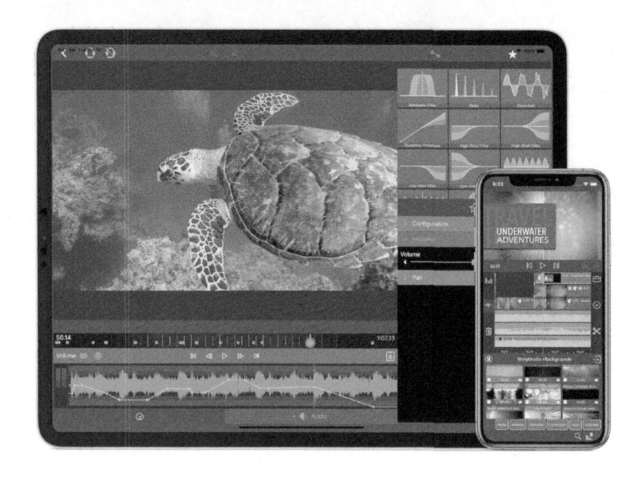

D. LumaFusion for iPad Pro

LumaFusion by LumaTouch is designed specifically for video editors wanting to edit video at a deeper level. The latest iPad Pro is a powerhouse for video editing, not only because you are mobile, but you're also able to use the bigger screen to craft even better videos. With the added power of the iPad Pro and the feature set of LumaFusion, you can compare the editing experience to editing on a MacBook or Mac Pro with Final Cut Pro.

It is a multi-track video editor similar to VideoLeap, with 3 layers of audio and 3 for video. You can load lots of different plugins and effects.

The new iPad Pro 2018 also has a USB-C port which enables you to bring in your footage from your DSLR and High-End cameras directly to the device as high as 4K shot on DSLR cameras. All of the apps mentioned above will also work on the iPad Pro.

With the introduction of iPad Pro in 2018, Apple did something unusual. They made this pro device that is fun to use and increased the power of the graphics card by 1,000% from the previous generation iPads. What does this mean? It speeds video processing, video editing, photo processing. Additionally, with the machine learning that's built into the iPad Pro, each time you perform a task it gets faster.

Some of the apps mentioned above for video editing depend entirely on what the output format is going to be. Also, how much editing and effects, captions, title text and graphics layers will go on top of your video. This is possible with apps like InShot and VideoLeap. iMovie has a particular limitation on how many text layers you can have on top of your video: you're only limited to one or two per section. In-shot lets you layer on text layers. You can even layer on stickers and animated graphics on your video. You can control when these come on the screen and when they go out.

E. Blackmagic DaVinci Resolve for iPad

DaVinci Resolve for iPad
DaVinci Resolve for iPad is the world's only solution that combines editing and color correction in one software tool! Its elegant, modern interface is fast to learn and easy for new users, yet powerful for professionals. DaVinci Resolve lets you work faster and at a higher quality because you don't have to learn multiple apps or switch software for different tasks. That means you can work with camera original quality images throughout the entire process. It's like having your own post production studio in a single app! Best of all, by learning DaVinci Resolve, you're learning how to use the exact same tools used by Hollywood professionals in high end post production studios!

Turn work around fast using cut page editing!
The cut page is perfect for projects with tight deadlines that you have to turn around quickly. It's also great for documentary work. The cut page has a streamlined interface that's fast to learn and designed for speed. Features such as source tape for visual media browsing, fast review, and smart editing tools help you work faster than ever. The sync bin and source overwrite tools are the fastest way to edit multicam programs, with easy-to-create perfectly synchronized cutaways! With DaVinci Resolve you'll spend more time editing and less time hunting for shots.

Hollywood's favorite color corrector!
The DaVinci Resolve for iPad color page is Hollywood's most advanced color corrector and has been used to color and finish more high-end feature films and television shows than any other system! It's also approachable with features designed to make it easier for new users to get great results while they continue to learn the advanced tools. For example, primary control sliders will be familiar to anyone who's used image editing software, making it easy to adjust contrast, temperature, mid-tone detail, saturation and more. The color page has an incredible range of primary and secondary color grading features including PowerWindows™, qualifiers, 3D trackers, advanced HDR grading tools and more!

Blackmagic Cloud Collaboration

DaVinci Resolve for iPad supports the revolutionary Blackmagic Cloud, a whole new way of collaborating using cloud based workflows. Simply create a Blackmagic Cloud ID to log into the DaVinci Resolve Project Server and set up a project library for your project. You can assign any number of collaborators to a project, using Blackmagic Cloud to share projects. Multiple people can work on the same timeline! When changes are made, you can see and accept them in the viewer, changes are only applied when you accept updates. A single click can relink files, update timelines, or view changes. Built-in timeline compare tools let you merge changes into a master timeline so others can continue with edits.

AI Tools for Creativity

DaVinci Resolve features cutting-edge AI processing powered by the DaVinci Neural Engine. Tools such as magic masks need only a single stroke to locate and track people, features, and objects in a shot. You can make characters stand out in an underlit shot, or invert the person mask and stylize the background. Smart reframing repurposes footage to dramatically different aspect ratios by recognizing the action in a scene and panning within it so you can quickly create a square or vertical version for posting to social media. Voice isolation lets you easily remove loud, undesirable sounds from interviews and dialogue recordings from noisy locations. AI tools create quick, accurate results saving you hours of time!

II. Hardware/Gear

The following are some of the hardware/ gear that I personally use for stabilization, audio recording, and illumination.

A. Audio Gear

There are several ways to record audio on your iPhone. Some of the gear is wired and others are wireless. To record audio, we use microphones, there are a few mics that are part of your iPhone but others can be wired or wireless and bring the audio much closer to your device.

Shotgun Microphones

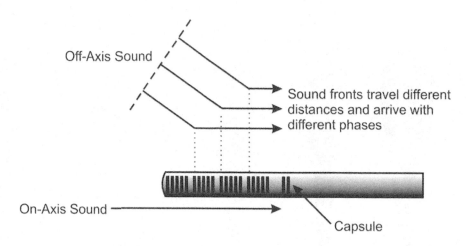

Image from: https://www.soundonsound.com/sound-advice/q-how-do-shotgun-mics-work

A shotgun microphone picks up audio in a very specific pattern and it is typically pointed in the same direction as the camera lens. The shotgun microphone can capture audio up to a certain distance. These microphones are industry standards as they're used in "boom" mic formation.

An external shotgun microphone does an excellent job; it may be attached to DSLRs, iPads or iPhones.

Here are a few models that make this possible and they're mainly used for dialog in TV shows and movies. Most shotgun microphones end in a 3.5mm plug that can connect to the iPhone through the Lightning to Headset adapter and have a super-cardioid pickup pattern. Here's a top-seller shotgun microphone shortlist to get you started:

- Rode VideoMicro Compact On-Camera Microphone ($59)
- Rode VideoMic Pro with Rycote Lyre Shockmount ($229)
- Sennheiser MKE 600 Shotgun ($329)

Lavalier Microphones

A lavalier microphone or LAV mic for short, is used mostly for interviews as the microphone is small.

Having a microphone attached to the speaker brings a higher level of audio to your device. Since the microphone is near the source of the sound the audio doesn't need much touch-up.

It comes in two varieties. A wired LAV mic usually comes with a 20-foot extension cable; this microphone can be attached to your shirt, blouse, or t-shirt, then the wire is fished through your shirt and attached to the camera via an extension cable.

A wireless LAV mic usually has a USB connection either to your computer for directly recording audio to your computer or your iPhone using a USB camera adapter. With this setup, you can get excellent audio wirelessly into your device while you're shooting video.

External Recorder

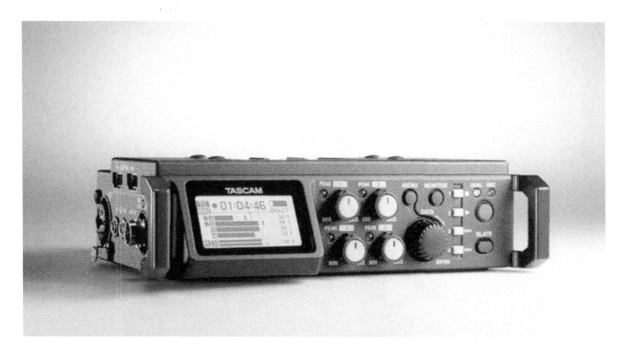

TASCAM DR-701D

The third way of recording audio is with an external audio recorder. I'll always recommend an external audio recorder as it works exceptionally well with multiple speakers and when you're doing interviews. This way you have separate audio tracks for each speaker, and you can apply audio effects to boost their sound the best way possible.

A setup with an external recorder and LAV mics will give you the most flexibility to capture high-quality audio. This audio can later be also used on a podcast. Combining audio from a recorder and bringing it together with the shot video requires higher-end apps such as FinalCut Pro, LumaFusion, and Adobe Premiere on your desktop/laptop machine. You would bring in your source files and lay out the tracks so that the audio track is synced with the video (usually the software is smart enough to properly mark them).

Direct Audio (Mobile Phone microphones)

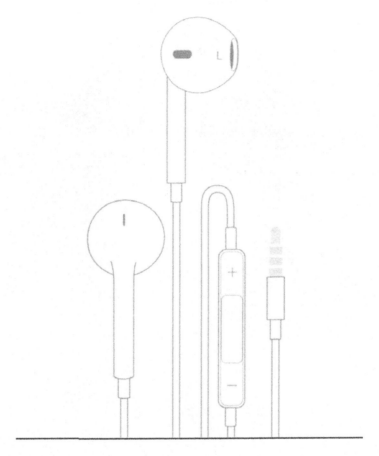

Image of airbuds

The fourth way to record audio is directly from your mobile device. As I mentioned earlier, these mobile devices usually have smart microphones that cancel out a lot of the ambient sound and elevate your voice as it's coming into the device, and the device is smart enough to isolate your audio from the ambiance.

B. Stabilization Equipment

There are several methods to stabilize your video. Having your device mounted to a stable gear is essential to capturing quality video.

Gimbal

A gimbal is a battery-powered device with motors on each of its 3-axes and a smart brain to keep your phone stable by adjusting the position of the phone in relation to how you're holding the device and your physical movements. Here's a list of some of the gimbals that can be your assistants in capturing your videos.

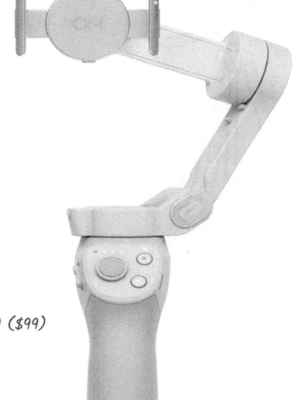

- DJI Osmo Mobile 4 (Shown on right) ($99)
- Smove Mobile ($159)
- Zhiyun Smooth 4 ($99)
- FREEFLY Movi ($299)

Tripod

A tripod is one of the oldest stabilization devices that's been around with us for a long time. The three legs make it the most stable device ever. They can range from very cheap to very expensive and are designed to hold very heavy equipment. Tripods also come with different types of heads that make it easier to pan and tilt with quite an ease. It comes down to the type of movement you're trying to capture. If you are your own cameraman, you'll be fine with the simplest tripod with a ball head. If you're recording video for someone else, you'll most likely be panning the camera left to right as the speaker moves or paces on the stage. Following are a few types of tripod heads that'll work with your tripod and camera:

- Ball Head
- Fluid Head
- Pistol Grips
- 3-Way Pan and Tilt Head
- Flexi Tilt

Each of the Tripod Heads offer a specific purpose while all the tripod heads offer pan and tilt. The Ball head is the most popular for photographers and videographers, but the Fluid Head features a "drag" which enables you to capture smooth panning shots.

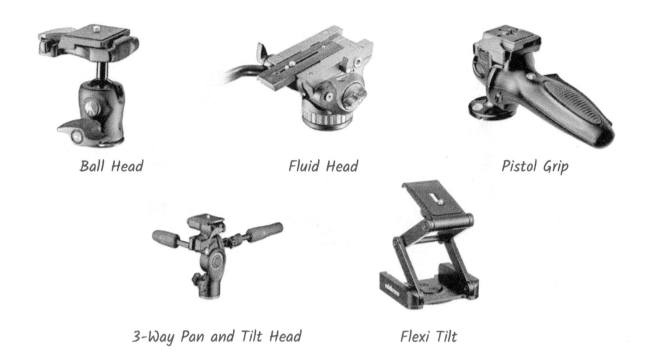

Ball Head   Fluid Head   Pistol Grip

3-Way Pan and Tilt Head   Flexi Tilt

I previously mentioned for stabilization you want to use devices like a three-axis gimbal or a tripod. There are, of course, other methods to stabilize video. What specific hardware do I recommend? For stabilizing video using your smartphone, you can use the DJI Osmo Mobile 2. It has a 15- hour battery life, and you can attach the phone and record your video in a stabilized fashion. You can be running with your camera gimbal, and your video footage comes out smooth as the three monitors on this device help stabilize the footage as you're recording it.

In addition to DJI Osmo Mobile, you've probably seen the ads for a Smove mobile device on Instagram and Facebook. The one advantage this device has over DJI is that it's got a built-in tripod stand and an extended arm. Both the DJI and the Smove mobile can track your subject automatically, and both devices work well with both iOS and Android.

C. Lighting Equipment

One way to achieve the best lighting for your video is to shoot it outdoors, particularly when there is plenty of cloud coverage, as this creates soft light. If shooting outdoors, it's best to use a diffuser and avoid standing in harsh sunlight. Instead, stand in the shade of a tree or building to avoid harsh shadows. Additionally, it's important to make sure the sun is not behind your subject. The sun should always be behind the camera so that your focal point, the subject, is illuminated and not the lens.

When filming indoors, it's important to use a lighting kit specifically designed for continuous lighting. This will provide a soft, natural-looking shadow and make your subject the focal point. These kits can be purchased for as little as $60 to $150, and typically include three box lights, a tripod, and light stands. It's important to arrange these lights correctly to ensure they are illuminating your subject and creating the desired look.

CONCLUSION:

This book is the 1st in my tech series. Next up you can read all about the next step on my journey - PODCASTING. When I was younger I wanted to be a pilot. It wasn't until that one day when I saw my Father sitting at the computer did I have a change of hea rt. He said let me show you how it's done and he did it with such amazing efficiency. I hope that as I show you how I did it that you will be able to achieve your dreams. I am Super Junaid. As you keep experimenting with video, I want to let you know that I can help you at all times. I am available on social media. For all inquiries, send me a message.

Made in the USA
Columbia, SC
24 October 2024

45029449R00037